C000181133

Cotswolds

Wet Nose Publishing Ltd

www.countrysidedogwalks.co.uk

First published in September 2016 by **Wet Nose Publishing Ltd**

All enquiries regarding sales telephone: 01824 704398
email cdw@wetnosepublishing.co.uk
www.countrysidedogwalks.co.uk
ISBN 978-0-9931923-6-4

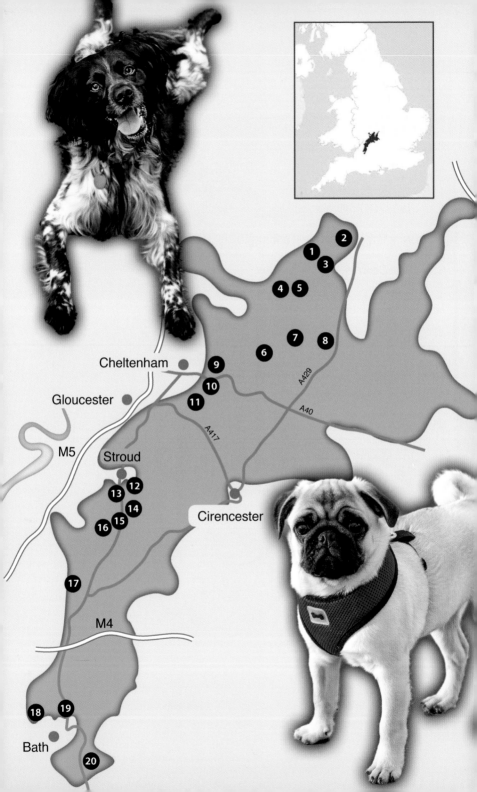

Cheltenham

Gloucester

M5

Stroud

Cirencester

A429

A40

A417

M4

Bath

1
2
3
4
5
6
7
8
9
10
11
12
13
14
15
16
17
18
19
20

Contents

Introduction

The twenty walks included in this book are all designed so that you and your wet nosed friend have a really enjoyable time. Where there are stiles, they are specially designed with lift gates for dogs. At a quick glance there is information at the beginning of each walk to tell you what to expect and what you may need to take with you. The descriptive guides will also warn of any roads ahead or areas of livestock so that you can get your dog on the lead well in advance.

Dogs just love to explore new places. They really enjoy the new smells and carry themselves a little higher with the added excitement. Going to new places gets you and your dog out and about, meeting new people and their dogs. It is important to socialise dogs, as they will be more likely to act in a friendly manner towards other dogs, as they gain confidence.

The stunning pictures in this book are just a taster of what you can see along the way. Many of the walks have fantastic views and scenery. Some of the walks are wooded, offering shade on those hot summer days.

The walks are graded Easy, Medium and Challenging. They are all around one to three hours long, depending on your and your dog's pace. You may start with the easy ones and work up to the challenging walks depending on your and your dog's fitness. Different dog breeds and dog age must be taken into account when you decide which walks to do.

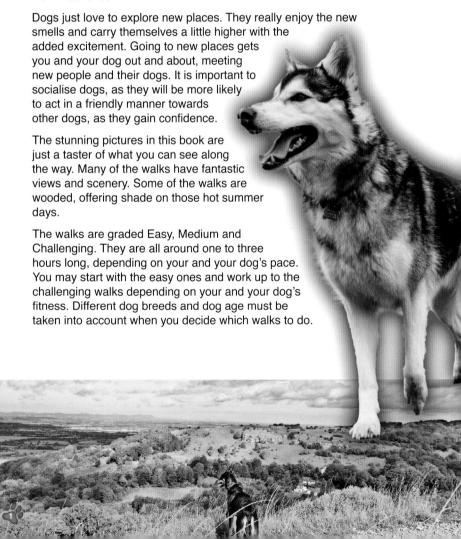

Different breeds of dog have different levels of fitness. For example, bulldogs can only do short walks whereas a border collie or a springer spaniel are extremely energetic and difficult to tire out. It is recommended that you do some research on the breed of dog that you own to get to know what sort of exercise that they require.

You may have a walk that you are happy doing with your dog every day, but this book will show you new areas to explore with a change of scenery and a chance to meet new people and their dogs. Dogs love new places to visit and you will see the change in them as they explore the new surroundings, taking in the new smells with delight. You will fulfil both your life and your dog's just by trying somewhere new.

Some of the walks include bridleways, so you may encounter horses and cyclists. It is important to put your dog on a lead if you see horses approach. It is always helpful to say hello to the riders as they near so that the horse realises that you are not a threat.

Ground Nesting Birds

Watch out for vulnerable ground nesting birds from the beginning of March until the end of July. Dogs that stray off the main paths may disturb birds and chicks, possibly killing them or breaking eggs. Species to look out for are Skylarks, Meadow pipits, Curlew, Red and Black grouse, Snipe and Pheasants.

Some if not all of these birds are declining in numbers, due partly to their vulnerability when nesting. Dogs are a threat to them, even if treading on them unintentionally. Some other threats are foxes, badgers, stoats, weasels, birds of prey and crows.

Please help to protect these birds during the nesting season by keeping your dog on the paths when walking in open areas such as grassland, moors, heathland and scrub.

Rivers

Some dogs love water and will think nothing of plunging into the river. With the extreme weather conditions over the last few years, a river that may be safe for your dog to swim in can change in a matter of hours to become a swollen torrent, that could wash your dog away. Please be careful when near rivers if there have been heavy periods of rain or if they look swollen or fast flowing. It is best to put your dogs on the lead, until you have assessed the situation.

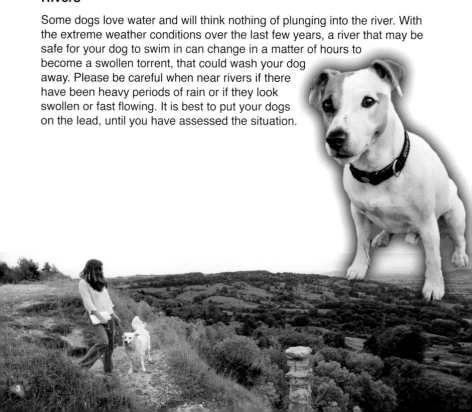

Livestock

If you find that you need to cross a field with cattle or horses and they seem interested in you or your dog it is recommended within the Countryside Code to let your dog off the lead. Never try to get between livestock and your dog. Your dog will get out of a situation a lot more easily with speed than you can. It is usually only cattle with young calves that are a threat, or young heifers or bullocks that tend to get a little inquisitive. They will usually stop when they get close to you or your dog.

Most horses will come over for a fuss but a small proportion do have a problem with dogs. They may see them as a threat and will act to defend the herd. Horses that are out with a rider are completely different as they are not defending the herd, and as long as you keep a safe distance there should not be a problem.

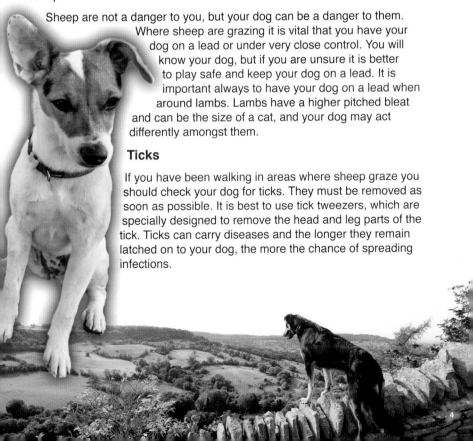

Sheep are not a danger to you, but your dog can be a danger to them. Where sheep are grazing it is vital that you have your dog on a lead or under very close control. You will know your dog, but if you are unsure it is better to play safe and keep your dog on a lead. It is important always to have your dog on a lead when around lambs. Lambs have a higher pitched bleat and can be the size of a cat, and your dog may act differently amongst them.

Ticks

If you have been walking in areas where sheep graze you should check your dog for ticks. They must be removed as soon as possible. It is best to use tick tweezers, which are specially designed to remove the head and leg parts of the tick. Ticks can carry diseases and the longer they remain latched on to your dog, the more the chance of spreading infections.

Forests

The forest walks in this book are a changing landscape, which makes them unique and interesting. Descriptions may change with time, for instance a path may be described as being in the shade of the forest, but as this is a worked forest a section could be clear felled at any time. Another change over the years could be where a view is described across a previously felled area. This could then be planted up and trees grown blocking the views. Paths may change but this is less likely. On rare occasions the Forestry Commission may temporarily close paths due to forest works but again this is even less likely on a weekend. Any changes to the path networks that may occur after the date of print will be updated on our website.

Does your dog fetch a stick?

Most dogs love sticks and will pick them up without any encouragement from their owners. Vets and dog trainers recommend that you should not throw sticks for dogs. They can cause nasty injuries, sometimes fatal as the stick can pierce the throat, or rebound off the ground and cause harm to your dog.

Please clean up after your dog

Always be prepared, having dog bags with you at all times. Once you have cleaned up after your dog, please keep the bag, until you see a bin. If there are no bins provided, then take it away with you to a roadside bin. Dog bags that are discarded on the paths or in the bushes are unpleasant, unsightly and will not degrade.

1. Dover's Hill

Medium - 1.5 miles - 1hr 30min

This is a wonderful circular walk. There are stunning views near the start of the walk on reaching the topograph. There are wonderful deciduous woodland, grass meadows and hilly pasture, with mature parkland trees. There may be livestock grazing but there are no roads.

How to get there – The car park is found on the outskirts of Chipping Campden. From Chipping Campden, follow the sign for Dover's Hill on Dyers Lane. Continue straight ahead at the crossroads, where you will find the car park shortly after on your right.

Grid Reference – SP 137395

Postcode – GL55 6UW

Parking – Free in the National Trust car park

Facilities – There are no facilities

You will need – Dog lead, dog bags and water for your dog

The Walk

❶ Keep your dog on a lead or under close control as there may be sheep grazing. Pass through the gate in the corner of the car park, next to the notice board. Continue straight ahead on the well-worn path through the field. You will reach a topograph on the ridge of a hill, where you will have wonderful views.

Face the views and turn right to continue along the ridge of the hill. You will pass a line of trees on your left. After the tree line there is hawthorn scrub. Continue with the views on your left of Evesham and the beautiful countryside which surrounds it. You will reach and then pass a trig point.

❷ On reaching the end of the field turn left, and continue on the edge of the field with mature trees and a stock fence on your right. Pass beside a stone wall for a short distance. Don't go through a gate ahead, but follow the worn path ahead and left. Descend some steps, and when you reach another gate don't go through it but turn left.

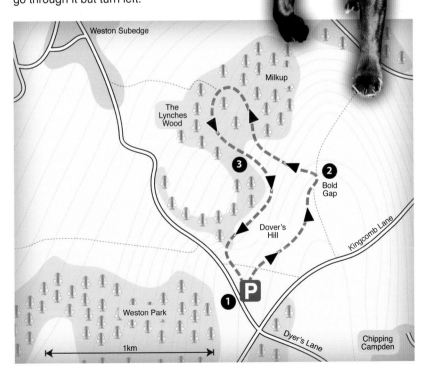

Descend on the edge of the field with trees and scrub on your right. Continue close to the field boundary on your right as you descend. You will pass a gate on your right, and continue to descend. On reaching the right hand corner of the field pass through the kissing gate and enter into mixed woodland. Continue straight ahead on the worn path. Ignore a path on your right soon after.

The path bends sharply to your left. You will cross a boardwalk where there are some mature sweet chestnut trees. You will now descend gently through the woodland. Ignore a path on your right, where you continue around another left bend. The path is level here and there is some thick laurel. You will ascend again, and there is a steep wooded slope on your right.

You will turn a sharp left bend and there is a series of steps. On reaching the top of the steps turn right on the level path. At the edge of the woods you will pass through a kissing gate. ❸ Continue straight ahead. Keep your dog on a lead or under close control. Stay close to the field edge on your right. The field slopes away ahead with mature parkland trees.

The path ascends as you reach the hill. As the path narrows stay close to the tree line on your right. You will reach a copse of trees where you continue to follow the worn path. You will soon be close to a stock fence on your right. Continue to ascend gently and on reaching an opening, near to the corner of the fence line, turn left.

The path is less distinct for a short section. Cross a more defined path and continue straight ahead ascending the hill. You will have views on your left and after passing between hillocks, you will reach a familiar spot at the topograph. Turn right to retrace your steps back to the car park.

2. Ebrington

Easy/Med - 3.5 miles - 2hrs

This wonderful circular walk takes you through quiet countryside. You will walk amongst arable fields, hedgerows and woodlands. Cross a meadow, where you will have views across a lake to the elegant manor house. Please note: from 1st October – 1st February it is shooting season, and gunfire may be heard in the area. If your dog is timid or wary of loud bangs, avoid this walk during the shooting season. There is a quiet road, and there may be livestock on parts of the walk. You will need to keep your dog on a lead for parts of the walk, as you near an area where pheasants are reared.

How to get there – Ebrington can be reached off the A429, between Warwick and Cirencester. Turn off the road on reaching the B4035, which is signed for Chipping Campden. On reaching a sharp left bend, continue straight ahead, following the sign for Charingworth and Ebrington. Continue on the road through Charingworth Village. On reaching the sign for Ebrington, continue on the road, until you reach road signs for Chipping Campden, Ebrington and in the opposite direction, Charingworth and Shipston-on-Stour. You can park just beyond the sign in the direction of Chipping Campden, beside the houses, and a water trough.

Grid Reference – SP 187400   **Postcode** – GL55 6NL
Parking – On the roadside, near to Home Farm House B&B
Facilities – There are no facilities
You will need – Dog lead, dog bags

The Walk

1 From the road, ascend out of the village, in the direction of Charingworth. Pass the road sign for Chipping Campden and a road on your left, which is a no through road, and then turn left immediately after. Continue on the sealed road, with a meadow on your left and a post and rail fence. There is also a meadow on your right. You will soon descend and pass houses on your far right.

Ascend gradually, past a woodland copse on your right and a hedgerow on your left. After you pass the woodland copse there is pasture and estate fencing on your right. There are views across to the hills in the distance.

Descend again and continue between estate fencing. The track bends sharply to your left, turn right here and continue on a grass path. You will reach a farm gate and a kissing gate. Pass through the kissing gate and continue on an obvious worn path through the middle of a field, with telegraph lines on your right. Keep your dog on the path, as there may be newly sown crops in the field.

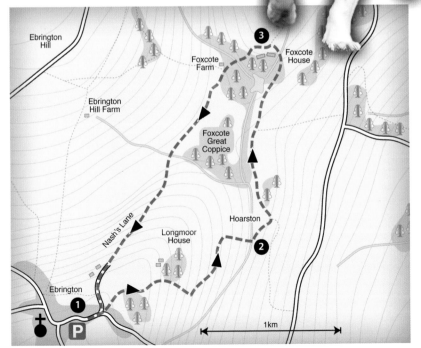

As you reach a hedgerow, which divides a large field, turn left and continue beside the hedgerow on your right. Continue on the edge of the field. You will begin to ascend gently as you near the end of the field. Pass through an un-gated entrance into another field and after roughly ten yards turn right.

Continue on the grass track, descending through the field. On reaching a hedgerow turn left and continue on the edge of the field. Ignore a gap in the hedgerow, which goes to another field. Continue for about fourteen yards and then turn right, where you will see a waymarker and a footbridge over a stream. Keep your dog on a lead, as there may be game birds in the area.

2 Cross the footbridge. As you pass through the gap in the hedgerow, you will see a pond on your left. Continue straight ahead, with a hedgerow on your right, and a stone barn on your far left. Continue straight ahead beside a hedgerow, where you will reach a stone track.

Turn left on the stone track and ascend. You will pass the stone barn on your left, which is used as a shooting lodge. Continue to follow the stone track, with a hedgerow on your right. As the track bends to your left, ignore a path on your right. Continue between hedgerows. Ignore a track on your left and continue straight ahead.

There is woodland on your left and arable fields on your right. Pass through a farm gate into pasture, keeping your dog on a lead or under close control. Continue straight ahead, leaving the track as it bends to your right. Continue on the edge of the field. Ignore a stile on your left, which enters into woodland.

As you see a farm gate on your left, you will see the impressive estate house and lake. Continue past the gate on your left, and head for another gate straight ahead. On reaching the farm gate pass through it, and continue between the stock fence and hedgerow.

You will pass a pheasant pen on your right and woodlands on your left. Beware of the electric fence beside the pheasant pen. After passing the pen you will have woodlands on both sides. Continue through the mixed broadleaved and conifer woodland, on the obvious worn path between the stock fences.

On reaching a track turn left. Descend gently, where you will reach a gate beside a cattle grid. Continue on the track, and ascend. You will reach a sealed access road, where you will reach several junctions. Continue straight ahead, and on reaching the main access road, turn left. You will pass close to the estate house on your left. **3**

Continue with the estate fence and hedge on your left. Ignore another access road on your right. Descend, and pass through a gate beside the cattle grid. Continue straight ahead, passing a pond on your right and a house on your

left. You ascend and pass another house on your right. Ignore a gate and bridleway on your right and continue on the road.

You will pass some agricultural buildings on your left. You will now leave the sealed road. Continue straight ahead on a stone track between hedgerows. The track bends to your left and then you will descend.

You will go round another bend, where you pass an entrance to a field on your right. There is a stream on your left, where your dog can get a drink. Continue straight ahead and pass beside a farm gate straight ahead. Just after you will see a stone 'Watery Gate'. Your dog can access water here on your right.

Continue to ascend on the track with the hedgerow on your left and a field on your right. Ascend the track on the edge of the field, where you will pass beside a hay barn and agricultural buildings. Continue on the farm track beside the arable field on your right. You will pass a track on your right, and on your left there is access to water for your dog. Continue straight ahead and put your dog on a lead, as there is a house and a road ahead.

On reaching the end of the field, pass through the gate. You will pass Ridge Cottage and Oakham Farm. Continue straight ahead on the access road, where you will pass several houses.

On reaching the end of the road turn right. Continue through the village where you will reach back to your car.

3. The Mile Drive

Easy - 3.2 miles - 1hr 30min

This linear walk is close to Chipping Campden and Broadway, and is an ideal walk to let your dog have some time off the lead, before going on to explore the village. After crossing a couple of fields, you will reach a path beside a long and narrow meadow, between hedgerows. There are views in places.

How to get there – From the M5 turn off at junction 9, following the signs for Evesham A46, and Tewkesbury A438. Continue on the A46 following signs for Evesham. Before you reach Evesham, follow the sign on the roundabout for Broadway. On reaching Broadway, follow the brown signs for Broadway Tower. Turn left following a brown sign for forest/ picnic, which is immediately after you reach the sign for Fishill Quarry and just before you reach Broadway Tower. The car park is just after you turn onto the road, on your left.

Grid Reference – SP 118369
Postcode - WR12 7LD
Parking – Free in the car park
Facilities – Toilets and picnic tables in the car park
You will need – Dog lead, dog bags and water for your dog

The Walk

❶ There is a road close by to begin with, so keep your dog on the lead. From the car park, face the notice board and turn right onto the wide grass path. You will pass a picnic area and ascend with some stone steps.

Go through the kissing gate on your right, just before reaching a flight of steps. Keep your dog under close control and cross the field, diagonally to your right on the worn path. There is a road ahead, so put your dog on a lead before reaching the end of the field.

Cross a low stone stile and then cross the road. Continue on a worn path, which diagonally cuts across the field. On reaching the end of the field, pass through the gap in the stone wall. Continue on the well-worn path across another field. You will reach another stone wall. Pass through the gap and turn left on the wide surfaced path.

The path is lined with trees on your left, and on your right there is a wide grass strip, followed by a line of trees. As you continue you will see views of patchwork hilly fields. A little further on, cross a track and then leave the surfaced track as it bends to your right. Continue straight ahead on the worn grass path along the narrow field.

❷ On reaching the end of the narrow field, you have reached the furthest point of your walk. Simply turn around and retrace your steps back to the car park.

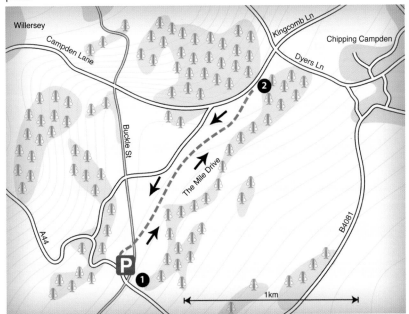

4. Stanton

Challenging - 4.1 miles - 2hrs 30min

This circular walk starts at the lovely, quiet, picturesque Stanton Village. The scenery is outstanding as you ascend through rough pasture, which has many mature trees and floristic grass hillocks. There are wonderful views after quite an ascent, but the ascent is mostly gradual. You will gradually descend through pasture, where you may encounter cattle, horses and sheep. There are some stiles which have dog lift gates. There is water in places, where your dog can get a drink. There are short sections of quiet village roads.

How to get there – From the M5 turn off at junction 9, following the signs for Evesham A46, and Tewkesbury A438. Continue on the A46 following signs for Evesham. Turn right where you see the sign for Dumbleton. Continue on the main road, and pass through Dumbleton. Stay on the road, and then turn left at the T-junction, following the sign for Evesham. Shortly after, take the next road on your right, signed Wormington. In Wormington Village turn right when you see the sign for Winchcombe and Cheltenham. On reaching the T-junction turn right on the B4632, following the sign for Cheltenham. Take the next road on your left, following the sign for Stanton. Continue on the road through the village, until you see the village car park on your left.

Grid Reference – SP 068341   **Postcode** – WR12 7NE
Parking – Free in Stanton Village car park
Facilities – There are no facilities
You will need – dog lead, dog bags

The Walk

1 From the car park, go to the road and turn right. Pass Stanton Court Cricket field on your right. Take the road on your left. Pass a war memorial on your left and then pass a fingerpost and follow the sign for Cotswold Way. Ignore a footpath on your left and ascend gently on the quiet road. At the bend in the road, take the road on your right, marked by the fingerpost for Cotswolds Way. **2** There is a stream here on your right, where your dog can get a drink.

Pass a thatched cottage on your right, veer to your left and follow a sign for Buckland. Continue now on a quiet lane. After you pass houses, continue between hedgerows with horse paddocks beyond. Ascend on the track, which is lined by trees. As you pass the paddocks, there is open grassland and scrub. Just before reaching a gate ahead, take a footpath on your right, which is waymarked for the Cotswold Way.

Descend to a gate and then ascend steps and pass through another gate, and follow the waymarkers for the Cotswold Way. Keep your dog under close control or on a lead, as there may be

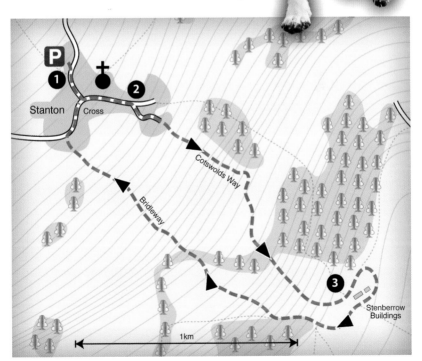

20

livestock. Continue on the well-worn path, beside a hilly meadow with some trees and scrub. Continue beside a line of trees on an undulating path. As you leave the tree line, you will ascend a little steeper. There are stunning views on your left, across the hilly landscape, with trees amongst the grassland.

You will reach a stile. Cross this using the lift gate for your dog. A stream flows beside the stile, where your dog can get a drink. Continue on the worn path, staying close to the tree line on your left, on the edge of hilly pasture. Pass a stone barn on your left and continue to ascend. If you stop to get your breath, look behind you, where you can enjoy wonderful views.

You will reach another stile on your left, with a lift gate for your dog. Cross the stile, and continue on the worn path. Veer to your right amongst hawthorn and scrubby grassland. Ascend on the well-worn path, with some mature ash trees, and gorse. The path will become very steep as you reach widely spaced mature ash trees. Veer to your left when you see a waymarker, and ascend some steps, where you will have views on your left. You will reach close to a house at the top of the hill. **❸**

Continue straight ahead; pass the gable end of the house on your right. Go through the kissing gate and continue straight ahead on a farm track through the middle of a field. Soon after, on reaching a fingerpost turn right. Put your dog on a lead and pass through a farm gate. Continue on a track, with trees on your right and a fence on your left, with a field beyond. Descend and pass between farm buildings. The path bends to your left, where you pass through another farm gate. Continue past the farm building on your right, and leave the track where it bends to your left. Continue straight ahead and pass a cottage on your right. Pass through a farm gate, and keep your dog under close control or on a lead, as there may be livestock grazing.

Stay on the field edge, with a tree line on your right. Pass through a farm gate and continue on the edge of another field, beside a stock fence and an old stone wall. As you descend, pass through another farm gate. Continue straight ahead, and follow the sign for the bridleway and not for the footpath. Cross rough grassland, on a worn grass track. You will reach a wood beyond the stone wall on your left, and outstanding views on your right and ahead. Pass through another gate and continue on a worn path across grassland. Descend across the middle of the field.

Pass through a gap of the remnants of an old hedgerow. Continue to descend and veer to your right on the worn path. You will reach and pass through another farm gate. Continue straight ahead across an open field. Stay on the worn path. Continue straight ahead, where the path becomes less defined, and make your way to the large stone ahead.

On reaching the stone, the path is well worn again, and sunken. Pass through a gate, and then turn left. Pass through another gate and continue beside a stock fence on your right. Turn right and continue close to the stock fence on your right. You will have wonderful views as you descend. On reaching gates at the end of the field, pass through the small one straight ahead. Continue straight ahead, beside a stock fence on your right. Pass beside a tree enclosure on your left. Descend quite steeply. You will reach the corner of the field. Pass through the second gate on your right. Follow the waymarker, ahead and to your left. You are now back on the Cotswold Way.

You will see a worn path as you continue. Head towards the houses, put your dog on a lead and pass through a gate, which is left of the houses. Turn left on the track, between yew hedges. On reaching a road turn right. Continue through the village, and stay on this road, where you will reach back to the car park on your left.

Countryside Dog Walks - Cotswolds

5. Broadway Tower

Challenging - 2 miles - 2hrs

This circular walk passes the magnificent Broadway Tower, which is the highest mini castle in the Cotswolds. You can enter the tower, but there is an admission fee. There are deer in the grounds beside the tower. You descend on the edge of quiet sloping pasture, with amazing views of the surrounding countryside. Cross the edge of a field, which has many hillocks. Your ascent is gradual, crossing fields to reach a quiet lane. There may be livestock and there is a quiet country lane.

How to get there – From the M5 turn off at junction 9, following the signs for Evesham A46, and Tewkesbury A438. Continue on the A46 following signs for Evesham. Before you reach Evesham, follow the sign on the roundabout for Broadway. Follow the brown signs for Broadway Tower.

Grid Reference – SP 111358
Nearest Postcode – WR12 7LB

Parking – Donation box. The car park closes at 5pm, but there is roadside parking

Facilities – A cafe is by the car park

You will need – Dog lead, dog bags and water for your dog

The Walk

❶ If you have parked on the road-side then take the entrance into Broadway and then take the gate immediately on your right. From the car park head back towards the yellow stone building, which is the café. Pass the café and notice board and continue towards the road. Just before reaching the road, go through the kissing gate on your left. Keep your dog on a lead or under close control, as there may be deer and sheep. Continue straight ahead on the well-made path, where you will reach the tower.

❷ The views are breathtaking on your left and ahead. As you reach the tower veer to your right and pass through another kissing gate. Turn left and continue on the Cotswold Way long distance route. Descend between the deer fencing and the stone wall. Pass through a small gate straight ahead and then descend on the edge of a field with a stone wall and stock fence on your right. There may be livestock grazing, so keep your dog under close control.

The views are fantastic ahead and to your right, Broadway Village can be seen surrounded by stunning countryside scenery. On reaching a small gate beside a more traditional stone stile, pass through it. Continue to descend on the edge of the field, and you will gain views on your left as you descend. Pass through another gate, and continue to descend on the edge of the field.

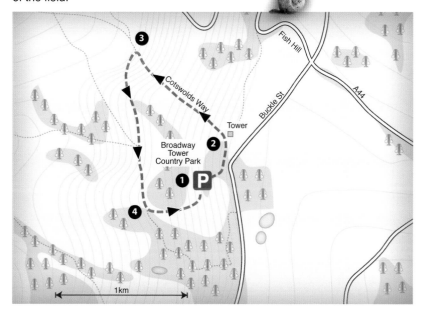

Pass through another gate beside a stone stile. On your left here there are benches, where you can sit and admire the beautiful scenery. Continue on the path as before on the edge of the field and descend the steps. The field here is undulating, with many small slopes. On nearing the end of the field you will reach a waymarker. ❸ Turn left here and continue across the field, close to the edge on a slightly sunken path.

There is a moderate ascent as you walk between hillocks and scattered hawthorn. You will have views on your right, where there are gaps in the trees. On reaching the end of the field, pass through the small gate and continue straight ahead. Continue on the slightly worn track and cross the field. There is a disused field boundary on your left, with the remains of a stone wall and a row of trees.

Follow the track, with views of the hilly countryside on your right. You will descend on the field edge, with a hawthorn hedge on your left. Pass through a small gate, beside the farm gate. Continue straight ahead, ignoring the path and track on your right. Pass under a copse of trees, between the stone wall and the stock fence. You will reach another small gate. Pass through the gate and continue on the grass track, and ascend towards a house.

Pass the house on your left, and soon after you will reach three lovely stone gate posts. Don't go through the gate, but turn left and pass through a small gate beside the farm gate. Ascend the stony track between the trees. As you continue there is a field on your right and coniferous trees on your left. Ensure you have your dog on a lead, as there is a road ahead and gardens.

You will reach a tarmac path. Continue straight ahead, where you will reach a quiet road. ❹ Turn left on the road and pass the houses on your left. Ascend on the road, where you will have estate fencing and trees on your right. On your left there are coniferous trees. As you near the top of the hill turn left, and pass through a kissing gate which is way-marked. Continue on the worn grass path, and soon you will see the café. Pass through the gate and turn right to reach the car park. If you have parked on the road continue straight ahead.

6. West Down & Wood   Medium - 3.1 miles 2hr

This circular walk begins at Cleeve Common. It has lovely views of the surrounding countryside, as you walk beside meadows. You will continue amongst lovely mixed broadleaved woodland. As you ascend gently, you will reach rough grassland and scrub, with wild flowers in the summer months. There may be livestock for short sections of the walk. There are no roads, other than the quiet access road for one house.

How to get there – From Cheltenham, continue on the A40 heading in the direction of Oxford. Turn off the dual carriageway, where you see the sign for Bourton Stow on the A436. Take the next road on your left, signed for Sevenhampton and Brockhampton. Turn right where you see the sign for Brockhampton, Charlton Abbots and Sevenhampton. Stay on the road and continue through part of Sevenhampton Village. Turn left at the cross roads, following the sign for Cleeve Hill Common. You will pass Deer Park Equestrian Centre on your right. Turn right at the T-junction, which is signed for Cleeve Common. Continue to the end of the road, where you will reach the car park.

Grid Reference – SP 009236
Postcode – GL54 5SR (Deer Park Equestrian Centre)
Parking – Free
Facilities – There are no facilities
You will need – Dog lead, dog bags and water for your dog

The Walk

❶ From the car park, continue on the wide grass path at the furthest end of the car park from the road. Continue past the entrance to Cleeve Commons and go straight ahead, on the red dirt track. The common is on your left, beyond the stock fence. There is scrub on your right. After passing the stock fence on your left and the scrub on your right, the area opens up with lovely views. There are now meadows on your left and right.

Continue on this track, and descend towards stone barns. There is a short ascent before you reach the barns. Just before you reach the barns take the footpath on your right, and pass the barns on your left. **❷** There is an open meadow on your right. You will have mixed broadleaved woodland over on your left. Descend gradually on the narrow path, with a stone wall on your left. Continue straight ahead, where you now leave the stone wall and pass between trees.

Pass a track on your left, and ascend the hillside. After leaving the trees the path bends to your right, where you now have trees on your right, and a meadow on your left, which is fenced. After passing the meadow keep your dog on a lead, or under close control before you reach a house and out buildings. Pass the house

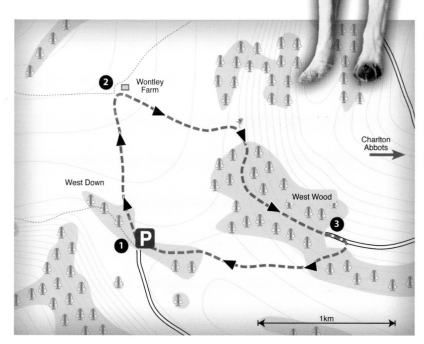

and continue on the sealed access road. Ignore a track on your right and continue on the road for some distance. There is a long, narrow meadow on your left and woodland on your right.

You will eventually reach a house on your left and pass through a gate ahead. Continue on the quiet road, between hedgerows. ❸ Soon after turn right, when you see the fingerpost for Sabrina Way. Continue between fields and hedgerows. After an opening, continue on the stony track, which ascends quite steeply through woodland.

Ignore a path on your right and continue straight ahead. As you get higher you will reach and walk beside a stone wall on your left, with a meadow beyond it. As the path levels the woods narrow significantly, and there is also a meadow beyond the trees on your right. As you continue the path splits. Take the path on your left, which is wider. Both paths run parallel for some distance. You will reach a scrubby open grass area. Ignore a path which veers to your left, and continue straight ahead.

The path ascends gradually, and as you continue you will reach a familiar path with the interpretation panel for Cleeve Common. Turn left here, where you will reach the car park.

7. Guiting Wood

Med - 2.7 miles - 2hrs

This circular walk has a beautiful clear river, where your dog can cool off and get a drink on hot days. You will walk amongst mixed broadleaved woodland for most of the walk on an undulating path. There is a section of quiet road, but you are still amongst the woodland. You will cross a small section of pasture, where livestock may be grazing. You may hear gun shots in the area, as there is a pheasant shoot close by, in the months between October and February. On passing through the estate woodland, please keep your dog on the footpath as there may be pheasants in the area.

How to get there – From Cheltenham, follow the signs for Prestbury, and then take the B4632, following the sign for Winchcombe. Continue on the road, through the middle of the village. Pass the square and a cross, and then after you pass the Methodist Church turn right on Castle Street. Continue on the road for about 4 miles. On reaching a cross roads, turn left following a sign for Kineton. You may have to pass through a gate on this road. The car park will be on your left off the road, and within a stone wall.

Grid reference – SP 086258   **Postcode** - GL54 5UZ

Parking – Free in the car park on Critchford Lane

Facilities – There are no facilities

You will need – Dog lead and dog bags

The Walk

❶ From the car park, walk to the road and take the track on the opposite side. Descend with a sloped grass hill on your left and a manor house on your far left. Pass a footpath on your left at the bend in the road. Continue on the tarmac track, following the sign on the fingerpost for Winchcombe Way. Pass a house just after 'Pump Bottom Cottage'.

Ascend for a short distance with a hedgerow on your left and woodland on your right. You will soon descend and there is a river below the bank on your right. There are a couple of easy access points for your dog to reach the river a little further along. Soon there will be woods on both sides. Ignore a track on your left, which ascends into the woods. Ignore a path with a gate on your left a little further on.

You will walk between a stock fence and a post and rail fence. Ignore a path on your right and begin to ascend. Keep your dog under close

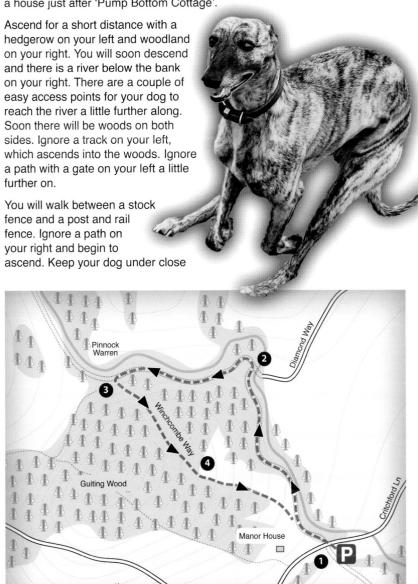

control now, as there is a quiet road ahead. You will reach close to the river which has crystal clear water, ideal for a hot dog to cool down.

❷ On reaching the road turn left, and ascend beneath the shade of the trees. The road levels off for a while and then you will descend. Continue on the road between the stock fences, with woodland on both sides. Pass a gate on your right and then on your left for Farmcote Estate. The road has a series of gradual ascents and descents. ❸ On reaching a fingerpost on your left at the bend in the road, pass through the kissing gate and follow the sign for Winchcombe Way. Pheasants are reared in the woodland, so please keep your dog on the footpath. Ascend between the banks in woodland. Your ascent becomes quite steep for a short section. The path becomes undulating and is sunken.

The woodland is mixed, with some hazel coppice. Ignore a path on your left and right, and continue straight ahead. Cross a track and continue. There is less light as your reach a mature conifer plantation on your left. After passing the plantation there is a field on your left, beyond a hedgerow. The woodland continues on your right. The path becomes enclosed and narrow.

You will reach a kissing gate. ❹ Pass through the kissing gate and descend, keeping your dog under close control as you pass through an area of pasture, where there may be livestock. Continue on the edge of grassland. Pass through another kissing gate, and continue on the edge of the hilly field. You will meet a farm track after passing a house on your left. On reaching the track turn right and retrace your steps back to the car park.

8. Foxholes

Easy - 2.5 miles - 1hr 30min

This is a brilliant circular walk for you and your dog, as there are no roads and it is free of livestock. Much of the walk is in woodland, so there is plenty of shade to keep your dog cool on those hot summer days. Parts of the walk pass along the edge of arable fields. Whilst in the Wildlife Trust site you are asked to keep your dog on a lead. There are some bridleways, therefore you may encounter horse riders.

How to get there – From the A44 in Chipping Norton, take the A361 signed for Burford. Continue on this road, where you go over a railway crossing. Continue through the village of Shipton-under-Wychwood. On reaching a sharp left bend, turn right, following the sign for Milton-under-Wychwood. Continue through the village, and after passing a sports field on your right, turn right following the sign for Lynham and Kingham, on Church Road. At the end of the road turn right, following the sign for Bruern. Take a road/track on your left, which has a 'No Through Road' sign. Continue on this track, where you will eventually see the small car park on your left.

Grid Reference – SP 259207
Postcode – OX7 6QD
Parking – Free
Facilities – There are no facilities
You will need – Dog lead, dog bags and water for your dog

The Walk

❶ Leave the car park, cross the access track and continue straight ahead on a track between stock fence and hedgerow. Keep your dog under close control, as there are garden entrances on your right. Pass close to a house on your right. Pass through a kissing gate straight ahead and continue on the path, with stock fence and field on your left and a house and grounds on your right.

You will reach woodland on your right, and the path has bracken on both sides. Ignore a gate on your left and continue on the edge of the mixed broadleaved woodland. **❷** On reaching a junction of paths veer to your left, past a wooden barrier into the nature reserve. You are now on a bridleway, so beware of horse riders. The path ascends gently. Continue straight ahead, passing another barrier into the reserve on your right.

You will reach another junction of paths with a barrier into the nature reserve. Turn left here (before the barrier) and continue on the well-worn path. You will pass another barrier on your right. At the end

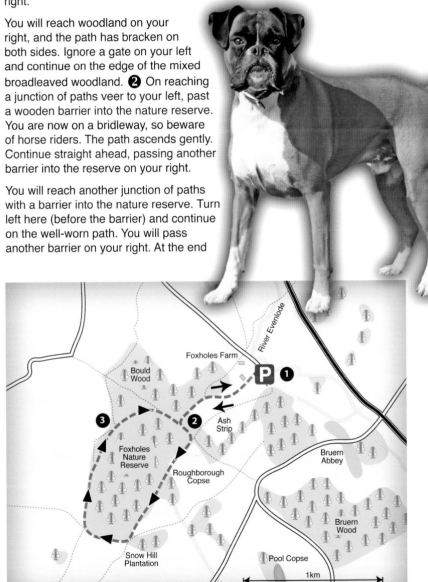

of the track you will reach a field. Turn right here, and continue on the edge of the field, with woodland on your right. There are views on your left across the hilly landscape. On reaching the corner of the field, continue straight ahead.

Descend gently along a woodland ride, with grasses and flowers growing on each side of the path. There is a ditch on your right. You will cross a track and continue straight ahead. As you continue, ignore another track on your right, which has a cattle grid. Shortly after you will reach a track, which joins from your left. Join this track, continuing straight ahead. Soon after, the track bends sharply to your right. You now continue on the edge of a field, with the woodland edge on your right.

Ignore a track into the woods on your right and continue straight ahead. Just before you reach the corner of the field, take the footpath on your right (not the second right). Continue on the woodland edge, with a line of trees on your left and a field beyond. The path bends sharply right, as you pass a waymarker. Turn left soon after, again this path is way-marked. Continue close to the woodland edge.

After about 20-30 minutes, ignore a footpath on your right and continue on the woodland edge. Pass another waymarker where another path joins, and continue straight ahead. Just after you will pass over a dip and then turn right. You reach an interpretation panel. ❸ Turn left as you face the panel. Ignore a path on your left just after, and continue straight ahead on the narrow path between the bramble.

You will reach another reserve barrier. Pass through the barrier and turn right. Silver birch and oak dominate the woodland here. On reaching a bench and another barrier, turn left on a familiar path. Pass another barrier on your left and continue straight ahead, descending on the familiar path on the woodland edge. On reaching another barrier on your left, turn right, and continue on the woodland edge. Continue on this familiar path, where you will pass gardens on your left. On reaching a track, cross over and enter into the car park.

9. Devil's Chimney

Challenging - 1.5 miles - 2hr

This is a short but challenging circular walk, which passes an Iron Age hill fort, before walking along a cliff face, where on a clear day you will have fabulous views. You will then descend through wonderful broadleaved woodland, where you will reach Devil's Chimney, which is a limestone rock formation, and so named as it stands above a disused quarry like a tall chimney. There are steep descents and ascents on this walk. You may hear shooting in the distance at the start of the walk from a rifle range. Dogs that spook would be better on lead to begin with.

How to get there – This walk is situated between Cheltenham and Gloucester, off the A417. Join the A436 following the sign for Stow-on-the-Wold, and turn left almost immediately following the sign for Ullenwood. Take the second road on your right, Hartley Lane. Ignore the first car park on your left soon after, and just after you pass a house on your left, which has a lot of glass; take the track on your left. You will find the car park on your right.

Grid Reference – SO 950179
Postcode – GL53 9QW
Parking – Free (second along the road, not the first)
Facilities – There are no facilities
You will need – Dog lead, dog bags and water for your dog

The Walk

1 From the car park, go back onto the access road. Turn left and head towards the road. Take the footpath on your left, just before reaching the road ahead. Continue on the bridleway, with a row of trees on your right, and trees scrub and grassland on your left.

A little further along you will pass through a gate and continue straight ahead, between scrub and brambles. The area on your left is now fenced off, and there is rough grassland and scattered larch trees. There is scrub on your right, and as you continue you will see an exposed rock face.

There is exposed rock on the path in places. On reaching a gate, pass through it and turn left. **2** Follow the worn path between trees and scrub. You will soon pass amongst small hillocks, which are the remains of old quarry waste. Ignore a path on your right and continue straight ahead. You are now on part of the Cotswold Way long distance route.

Ignore any minor paths. You will ascend and then reach and cross over some exposed stone. The path widens now, and there are wild flowers amongst the grass and scrub in the summer months. Continue straight ahead on a dirt track, ignoring a sealed path on your left. Pass beside more hillocks on your right. You will reach and ascend onto an Iron Age hill fort. Keep your dog under close control or on a lead, as there is a cliff face ahead.

Pass a trig point on your far left. You will have views ahead and on your right. Keep to the edge of the hill fort with scrub on your right and open grassland on your left. You will reach a topograph, where you will have amazing panoramic views. Turn left and walk along the edge of the cliff face, keeping your dog on a lead.

Trees and hillocks will obscure your view. Descend on the path, where you will reach a fingerpost. ❸ Turn right, following the sign for Devil's Chimney, and continue to descend. The views are now on your left, as you switch back on yourself. Look out for the railings on your left, where you will view Devil's Chimney.

Continue on the level path, on the edge of the wooded hillside. After passing a bench on your left, you will descend quite steeply. You will pass a ruined building on your right. Soon after (about 20m) pass a mile stone, and then turn right.

❹ There is now quite a steep ascent on a wooded hillside. Stay on the path on your right, not the path on your left, which runs parallel for a while. The path will become sunken as you continue. Where the path levels out a little, cross another path and continue straight ahead. You will reach a stock fence on your left. Continue beside the stock fence. As you continue you will pass a gate on your left and then cross another path. You are now at a familiar spot. Go through the gate straight ahead, and then turn right.

Continue on the well-made path, between stock fences. There is a field on your left and scrub on your right. On reaching another path, turn left. Continue on a sealed track, between the stock fences and fields. Go through a gate and keep your dog under close control, as there are no boundary fences. Continue straight ahead, heading towards the agricultural buildings.

Continue on the track, past the agricultural building on your right. Turn left, and you will soon reach back to the car park.

10. Crickley Hill

Easy - 1.6 miles - 1hr 30min

This circular walk crosses over grassland, which in parts has small hillocks, which are the remains of old quarry waste and are reclaimed by nature. In the summer months the grassland areas are quite floristic. There are some wonderful views in places. Some of the paths are on part of the Cotswold Way long distance route. You will pass through woodland, where you can enjoy the shade on a hot day. There may be cattle on the walk, but they are a quiet breed, and are used to the many dog walkers who use the area. There are no roads.

How to get there – The park is situated between Cheltenham and Gloucester, off the A417. Join the A436 and follow the sign for Stow-on-the-Wold, and turn left almost immediately following the sign for Ullenwood. Turn left where you see the sign for Crickley Hill Country Park soon after.

Grid Reference – SO 928162
Postcode – GL4 8JY

Parking – Pay and display

Facilities – Toilets and picnic benches

You will need – Dog lead, dog bags and water for your dog

The Walk

❶ From the visitor centre go to the access road and turn left. Just before the road descends, take the gate on your left following the sign for Cotswold Way. Continue on the sealed path between the trees. You will reach a picnic bench and see wonderful extensive views on your right.

You will leave the shade of the trees and enter into open hilly grassland. Pass an interpretation panel on your left, and cross a mown grass area. Ignore a kissing gate on your left. The views continue on your right. Veer to your left and pass a farm gate on your left. You will now walk beside a stock fence on your left, where you can enjoy the views on a clear day.

You will pass amongst some small hillocks, which are the remains of old disused quarry waste, and now reclaimed by nature. On reaching a stone wall, go through the gate on your left. **❷** Descend on the stone path, which undulates between the hillocks. Continue beside the stone wall, ignoring a path which veers to your left.

You will reach and pass through a gate. As you enter the woods continue straight ahead, remaining on the

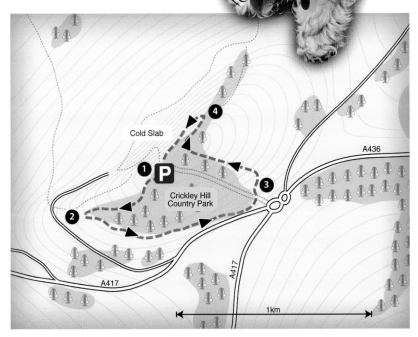

Cotswold Way, on a path at the edge of woodland. The path will veer away from the boundary fence. You will pass a chicken wire fence on your left. On reaching the end of the chicken wire fence veer to your right, following a waymarker. Beech trees dominate the woodland here.

You will see a gate ahead. Put your dog on a lead and pass through the gate. There is a busy road on your right. Continue on the path between the trees. The grass path becomes wide, and will veer to your left. Cross a grass track and then go through the gate. You have now left the Cotswold Way.

Please keep your dog under close control, as there may be livestock grazing and there is an access road ahead. If there are cattle, they are a gentle breed and are used to dogs and walkers. Follow the red waymarker, and continue straight ahead. There are mature parkland oak trees on your left. On your right there is a stock fence and cricket pitch.

❸ Cross the access road and continue straight ahead on the worn grass track. You will ascend gently on the path, which will veer slightly to your left. You will reach and continue beside a stock fence. Pass through a gate on your left, where you enter into Ochala Wood, and continue straight ahead on the stone path.

You will ascend for a short distance between trees. Ignore a path on your left and right, and continue to follow the red waymarker. Ignore another path on your left and continue straight ahead. On reaching estate fencing, do not go through the gate but turn left and continue beside the fence on your right. You will ascend gradually amongst the beech trees.

You will join another path and continue straight ahead. You will reach and then continue beside a stone wall. Pass through a gate on your right (not the one straight ahead) and follow the path through the woods. You will reach the woodland edge and turn left on the grass path. ❹ There are amazing, extensive views now on your right. On reaching a kissing gate put your dog on the lead, and pass through the gate and turn right into the car park. The visitor centre is just beyond the car park.

11. Cooper's Hill
Challenging - 1.5 miles - 1hr 30min

This wonderful short circular walk has fantastic views near the beginning, after a short but steep ascent. There are clearings in the broadleaved woodland, where you will pass amongst several hillocks, which are the remains of disused quarry waste. The hillocks have been reclaimed by nature and are covered in grass and heather. Some of the walk is on part of the Cotswold Way long distance route. There are no roads and no livestock.

How to get there – From the M5 take the turn off at junction 11A following the sign for London and Cirencester A417. Turn off the A417 when you see the sign for A46 Cheltenham and Stroud. At the roundabout turn right, following for Stroud. At the next roundabout continue straight ahead following for Stroud. Continue on this road for about 1 mile, and then turn left following the sign for Cooper's Hill. Continue on this road until you reach a 'No Through Road' sign. You will see the car park on your right.

Grid Reference – SO 891148
Postcode – GL3 4SB

Parking – Free in the car park

Facilities – There are no facilities

You will need – Dog lead, dog bags and water for your dog

The Walk

❶ From the car park, face the road and turn left. Continue straight ahead and ascend on the well-worn path. Pass through a kissing gate and enter Cooper's Hill Local Nature Reserve. You are now on part of the Cotswold Way long distance path.

There are views on your right, where the trees allow. Continue to ascend on the woodland path, which cuts through the hillside. You will reach a level section, where there is exposed rock on your left. Continue a little further and then turn left, following the waymarker for the Cotswold Way and ascend once again.

Soon after, follow the path which bends to your left. You will ascend quite steeply now. On reaching a clearing, you will have fabulous views on your left. **❷** Veer to your right, and then take the immediate path on your left, which ascends. You have now left the Cotswolds Way. Cross a grass track, and continue to ascend. You will pass over a series of hillocks, which have been formed from old disused quarry waste.

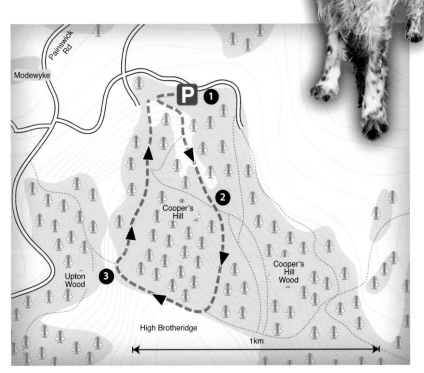

Continue through the woods on the undulating path. Just before the path narrows, with deep ruts on the left, veer to your right. Continue on the wide path, ignoring any minor paths on your left and right. You will soon reach a dilapidated old stone wall over on your left.

Continue beside the stone wall, until you reach an old vehicle barrier on your left. Turn right here and ascend gently. You will soon descend, and the path will turn sharply to your right. Ignore a sharp right turn and continue to descend as the path narrows. Continue on the path, descending on the edge of the woods. The path will become sunken for a short distance. You will reach another path.

❸ Turn right now, and continue once again on the Cotswold Way. On reaching another path, turn right and then left, following the waymarker for the Cotswold Way. Ascend on the path, which is quite steep to begin with. Veer to your left, where you will reach a familiar spot at the viewpoint. Face the view, at the waymarker and turn left. Follow the waymarker for the Cotswold Way, and retrace your steps back to the car park.

12. Rodborough Common   Easy - 1.2 miles - 1hr

This is a wonderful common, which is popular with local dog walkers. There are fabulous views, without the effort of a steep hill. The meadows are quite floristic in the summer months and there are scattered trees and scrub. There may be livestock grazing at certain times of the year.

How to get there – Rodborough Common is on the edge of Stroud. Take the A46 following the sign for Bath. Look out for the sign 'Parish of Rodborough' and then take the second road (with road markings) on your left, Rodborough Hill. Continue around a sharp left bend and soon after go over the cattle grid. Continue a little further, and the car park will be found just after you pass a road on your left signed for Mount Vernon.

Grid Reference – SO 851040

Postcode – GL5 5BL

Parking – Free in the car park

Facilities – There are no facilities

You will need – Dog lead, dog bags, water for your dog

The Walk

❶ From the car park ascend the slope and steps, which are opposite the car park entrance. Continue on the worn path, keeping your dog under close control, as there may be livestock grazing. There is also a road on your left. You will have wonderful panoramic views.

On meeting another grass path turn right. You should now be walking with your back to the road. Cross a wide grass track and continue straight ahead, heading towards a stone wall. On reaching the stone wall continue straight ahead, and walk beside the stone wall on your right.

As you continue there are new views ahead. Continue beside the stone wall, stopping roughly 100 yards before you reach a castle door. With your back to the wall, take the narrow path, which descends on your left. **❷**

Pass between old disused quarry workings and continue until you reach another wider path. Turn left on this path, and walk beside the small hillocks, which are the remains of disused quarry waste. Where the path splits into three, take the narrow path on your second right, which is the least obvious. Continue on the edge of the hillside.

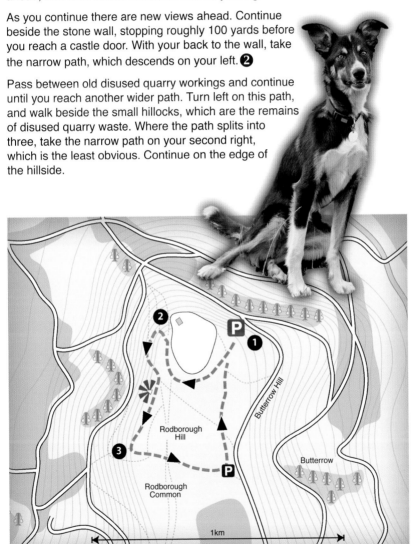

The path becomes more defined as you continue. You will pass more quarry workings as you continue. You will reach and then pass a small quarry face, which is fenced off. Just after passing the quarry face you will cross a narrow grass path. You will then join a wider path and continue straight ahead.

You will soon pass beside a stone wall on your right. Cross an entrance track, which leads to iron gates. Continue beside the stone wall and at the end of the stone wall continue straight ahead, staying on the edge of the hillside.

A little further along you will pass between scrub and bramble. You will have views again on your right, where you can look across Selsey Village and beyond. The views are amazing on a clear day across the horseshoe shaped hillside. Continue straight ahead, until nearing a stone wall over on your far left.

❸ Turn left here and ascend gently, where you will reach close to the corner of the stone wall. You will reach a wide grass track on your left. Cross this track and continue straight ahead, keeping the stone wall on your right. Pass a kissing gate on your right and continue on the wider path, which veers away from the stone wall.

Soon after, as the stone wall changes direction slightly, veer to your left, where you will join another wider path. There is a road in close proximity now, so keep your dog under close control or on a lead. Cross a wide stone track and veer to your left. There are car parks on your right and a road. You will reach another path. Cross this path which leads to a car park on your right and then join another wide grass path (turn 2nd left onto this path). You will see a familiar stone wall ahead and to your left. This track veers away from the road a little further along.

On reaching the trees and a fence turn right. Follow the narrow path over a series of hillocks. You will soon see the car park on your left. Continue on the path, descending the steps to reach the car park.

13. Cam Long Down Chall. - 1.8 miles - 1hr 30min

This circular walk begins on the edge of quiet woodland. You will be rewarded with amazing views and stunning scenery at the top of Cam Peak and Long Down. There may be cattle on areas of the walk, but they are used to seeing dog walkers. There are no roads.

How to get there – The walk is located close to Cam and Dursley. From the centre of Dursley follow the sign for the long stay car park. Pass the car park and continue on Drake Lane. At the end of Drake Lane turn right, following the sign for Ashmead and Coaley. Continue on Springhill, where you will find the car park on your right.

Grid Reference – Grid Reference

Nearest Postcode – GL11 5HG

Parking – Free in car park

Facilities – There are no facilities

You will need – Dog lead, dog bags and water for your dog

Countryside Dog Walks - Cotswolds

The Walk

1 Keep your dog under close control, as there may be cattle in the area. From the car park with your back to the road, take the gravel track ahead and to the right of the car park. There are houses on your far left. Head toward the house straight ahead. As you get close to the house, and before reaching the concrete track veer to your left. Pass a chain link fence on your left. Take the path which passes the chain link fence. There are marker posts, which will guide you on the path. There are some steps and you will have views on your left across the countryside to the River Severn and the hills beyond.

There is a field on your left, and mature oak trees and coppiced hazel on your right. The chain link fence is replaced with a barbed wire fence. Ascend gradually on the path. The views continue on your left, where the trees allow. After a spell of level ground, ascend some steps, where you will pass another marker post. The area is more open here, with scattered trees and sloping grassland on your right.

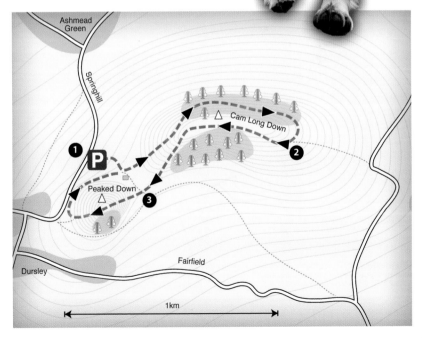

Soon after you will pass beneath the trees again. You will pass a gate on your left. Ascend for a short section quite steeply on the path, which has a handrail on your right. There is a stock fence on your left. ❷ Pass a stile on your left and turn right, where you join the Cotswold Way. The path ascends again quite steeply. Ignore the steps on your left and continue straight ahead.

The path has a series of switchbacks, which lessens the gradient. You will pass some mature ash trees, and then you will ascend above the tree line, where you will reach a waymarker. There are views in a new direction at this point. The small hill that you can see is Downham Hill. Continue past a waymarker on a worn path, which follows the ridge of the hill.

As you begin to descend slightly, you will see Peaked Down ahead, which is the grass dome. There are hillocks on your right, and views on your left and straight ahead. The path merges with another path from your right and behind. The path is wider now, and you will have views on both sides. The ridge becomes narrow, with sloped grassland on both sides. There is hilly landscape on your left, and flat landscape on your right, which stretches for miles.

Descend, and keep to your left, where you will enter into the woods. You will reach a fingerpost, which has six waymarkers. ❸ Continue straight ahead, following the sign for Cam Peak. Ascend to the peak, where you will have wonderful views once again. Choose your path back down to the car park, which can be seen from the top.

14.Coaley Peak

Medium - 3.4 miles - 2hrs

This circular walk has fabulous views at the beginning. The walk is predominantly amongst woodland. There are some steep ascents and descents on good tracks, following part of the Cotswold Way long distance route. There is a short section where you may be amongst livestock, and there is about 50 yards of busy road, where you walk on the grass verge.

How to get there – From Stroud, take the B4066, signed for Selsley and Uley. Just after you pass the sign for Nympsfield and Woodchester Park, turn right following the brown sign for viewpoint, picnic site and Nympsfield Long Barrow.

Grid Reference – SO 794014

Nearest Postcode – GL10 3TP

Parking – Free in the car park

Facilities – There are no facilities

You will need – Dog lead, dog bags and water for your dog

The Walk

❶ From the car park, face the view and take the first entrance to reach the field. Face the view again, and continue straight ahead. On reaching the edge of the field turn left, and continue straight ahead, beside the stock fence on your right. You will reach a kissing gate in the corner. Pass through the kissing gate, descend the steps and veer to your right. Pass over small hillocks, where you will then reach a topograph.

There are views across the countryside with the River Severn in the distance. Now go back towards the steps, but continue with the steps on your left and turn right. Follow the grass path at the edge of the hillside. Ignore a path on your left. You will pass a quarry face on your left and then you will reach a stock fence. Pass through the kissing gate and descend the steps.

You will pass through a woodland copse. Keep your dog under close control or on a lead as there is a road on your right, and there are no boundary fences. The quarry face can be seen on your left. Ignore a path on your right and continue straight ahead. Put your dog on a lead and ascend the stone steps, where you will reach the road.

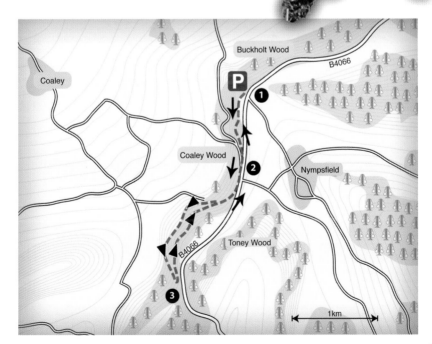

Cross the road and turn left. ❷ Continue straight ahead on the road for about 50m, following the waymarker for the Cotswold Way, and then turn right to enter into the woods. Descend steeply on a path through the wooded hillside. On reaching a fork, take the right path and continue to descend. You have now left the Cotswold Way.

The path will become sunken. Ignore a track on your left and continue to descend. You will reach a sealed access track near to a house. Don't take this track. Turn left following the footpath sign and ascend. Ignore a path on your left, which has a series of steps and continue straight ahead. The path is now fairly level.

Continue on the woodland edge, with fields on your right. Where the woods clear you will have views once more. Ignore a path on your right and then ignore a path on your left, and continue straight ahead. You will reach a stock fence. Turn left and continue on the edge of the woods, beside a field on your right. Ignore several paths on your left and continue beside the fields on your right. At the end of the path turn left on the track and ascend through the wood. Stay on the wide track, and ignore a track on your right.

On reaching another track, turn left and continue to ascend. When you are almost at the top of the hill turn left, ❸ following the sign for Cotswold Way. You will have views now on your left. You will descend slightly. Pass through a wooden barrier and descend. The path becomes undulating, and there is a quarry face on your right. The path levels out as you cut across steeply sloped woodland. You will have views on your left, where the trees have been cleared for the power lines.

Descend to reach another path and turn right. Go through a kissing gate and continue straight ahead on a level path. Ferns carpet the woodland floor here. You will descend again to reach another kissing gate. Pass through the kissing gate and continue straight ahead ascending on the path. Ignore a path on your left. You are now on a familiar path. Ascend steeply to retrace your steps, keeping your dog under close control or on a lead, as there is a road ahead, with no boundary fence.

On reaching the road turn left. On reaching the road junction continue to descend on your left. Cross to the other side when it is safe to do so. Turn right on reaching the fingerpost. Retrace your steps back to the car park.

15. Shortwood

Easy - 1.2 miles - 1hr

This short circular walk crosses over pasture, with small hillocks in places. There are outstanding panoramic views. On your return you will walk along the head of a valley. There may be livestock throughout this walk, and ground nesting birds from April until the end of July. There are no roads.

How to get there – From Stroud follow the signs for sports centre and then Whiteshill. Continue on the main road, through Whiteshill. On reaching a sharp right hand bend, turn left following the sign for Haresfield. Shortly after you pass a road on your right, you will reach the car park on your left.

Grid Reference – SO 831085

Nearest Postcode – GL6 6PP

Parking – Free in Shortwood car park

Facilities – There are no facilities

You will need – Dog leads, dog bags and water for your dog

The Walk

❶ Pass through the gate in the right hand corner of the car park if you are facing away from the road. Turn right and continue on the worn grass path. You will continue near to a stone wall over on your right. There are wonderful views on your left on a clear day.

As the track is about to descend and you reach a grass track veer left. You will now cross the meadow. Continue through the meadow, where you will reach a topograph.

❷ Here you will have amazing views across to the River Severn and beyond to hills in the far distance.

Continue straight ahead, passing the topograph and descend on the grass track, which has wheel ruts. There are many small hills, which are the remains of disused quarry waste. Continue on the wide grass track, which will veer to your left to reach a line of trees.

Haresfield
Beacon

Bunker's Bank

Shortwood

P

❶

❷

△

Haresfield
Topograph

❸

Standish
Wood

Standish
Park

Standish
Park Farm

1km

66

When you reach the line of trees veer to your right, and pass a bench on your far right. There are wonderful views across steep-sloping fields to the River Severn. Continue to descend and take a narrow path on your left, which crosses a ditch like feature. You will reach a bench just as the tree line ends. ❸ Turn around and take the narrow path which follows the line of trees, which are now on your left.

Ascend on this path, and after passing some trees on your right you will have views into the valley, with woodland on the opposite side. You will move away from the tree line for a short distance. On reaching the tree line on your left once again, take the path which veers to your right.

You will walk through sloped grassland, with a fence on your right for about 50 yards. There are some mature trees and hawthorn scrub. Stay close to the hawthorn on your left. The path narrows as you walk between scrub and becomes undulating. You will pass alongside a row of mature beech trees on your left, and there is woodland on your right.

Ascend slightly, where you will reach another narrow path. Turn right on this path and continue to the car park.

16. Stinchcombe Hill

Easy - 1.7 miles - 1hr

This is a delightful circular walk on top of Stinchcombe Hill, which is just outside Dursley. There are views in many places, without the need for an ascent. You will circle around part of Stinchcombe Golf Course. The course is screened off by trees and scrub, therefore for most parts you wouldn't know it was there. There are no roads or livestock, but you will have to cross a short section of the golf course.

How to get there – From Dursley, which is a market town in Gloucestershire, follow the sign for Stinchcombe Golf Course.

Grid Reference – ST 744983

Nearest Postcode – GL11 6AQ

Parking – Free in car park. Ignore the first car park on your right, which is for the golf course, and park at second car park on your left.

Facilities – There are no facilities

You will need – Dog lead, dog bags and water for your dog

The Walk

❶ From the middle of the car park, with your back to the golf course, pass a bench and descend for about 10 yards until you reach a narrow path. Turn right on the path, which cuts across the hillside. Another narrow path joins the path which you are on from your right. You will pass trees and scrub along the path, which will obscure your view in places.

You will reach a waymarker. Follow the Cotswold Way and join another path. Veer to your left and enter into woodland, on a wider path. Ascend. You will reach a fingerpost as you leave the woods. Turn right and keep your dog under close control or on a lead, as you will be close to a putting area. Continue on the path where you will pass another waymarker. Continue straight ahead on a narrow path, which cuts across the hillside. On reaching another waymarker, keep your dog under close control, turn right, and ascend briefly where you will reach the edge of the golf course. Almost immediately you will pass between scrub, which acts as a barrier for the golf course.

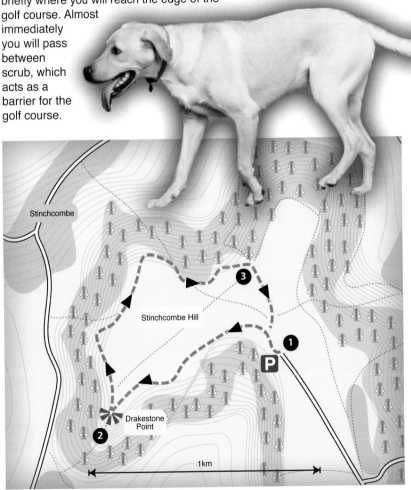

Continue on a narrow path, where you will pass another waymarker. You will once again have views as you continue in the open. Pass a fingerpost and continue, where you will reach a lovely double-sided stone bench. ❷ Now take the path which is parallel to the path you have walked, and head for the trig point. Pass the fingerpost again, where you will have views on your left.

Where the paths split, keep to your left. Pass the trig point over on your right. Just after the trig point, there is a topograph which will direct your views. Continue on the path with views to the River Severn and the distant hills. Keep your dog under close control and descend on the path between scrub. You will touch briefly with the golf course again.

After you pass some trees on your left you will reach a delightful stone shelter, where you can sit and enjoy the views of multi-coloured fields, hedgerows, woodland and the River Severn. With the shelter on your right, and your back to the view, continue on the path through the wood, with the golf course on your right. Shortly afterwards, ignore a path on your right. Continue through the wood, which will put more distance between you and the golf course. There is a dilapidated stone wall on your left.

Ignore a path on your left and continue straight ahead. You will pass a path on your right, and the Cotswold Way will re-join the path which you are on. Keep your dog under close control, ignore another path on your left where you pass a waymarker, and continue straight ahead. You will pass the golf course briefly. The path will widen and scrub will screen the golf course. You will reach the golf course again soon after.

❸ On reaching the golf course cross straight ahead, with care. Pass a standing stone on your right. You will reach a path, where you turn right. Continue on the edge of the golf course on your right, with woods on your left. On reaching a sealed track turn right. Continue on the track, taking care to watch for played golf balls as you pass the tee off. You will soon see and then reach the car park.

17. Lower Woods

Easy - 1.5 miles - 1hr

This circular walk is ideal on hot days, where you and your dog can enjoy the shade from the lovely broadleaved woodland. There are good tracks through the woodland. Hazel coppice and woodland rides allow light to penetrate the woodland in places. There are no roads or livestock

How to get there – Lower Wood is on the edge of Inglestone Common. From the M5 leave at junction 14, which is signed for Dursley. Continue on the B4509, signed for Wotton-Under-Edge. Turn right on the roundabout and follow the sign for Wickwar. Turn next left, staying on the B4509, following for Wickwar. At the end of the road, turn left signed for Trading Estate and Old Cider Mill. Turn right beside a car park, following the sign for Inglestone Common and Hawkesbury. Cross over a cattle grid, pass a track on your right almost immediately and then park on the edge of the common.

Grid Reference – ST 745887   **Postcode** – GL9 1BX

Parking – Free just beyond the cattle grid on the edge of the common (parking is permitted within 10ft from the road)

Facilities – There are no facilities

You will need – Dog lead, dog bags and water for your dog

The Walk

❶ Continue on the road for a short distance. Take the track on your right, which is opposite Richmond House on your left. Pass through the small gate, beside the farm gate into the Wildlife Trust nature reserve. Continue on the grass track, through mixed broadleaved trees. A little further along cross a track. Continue straight ahead and ascend gently.

On reaching another track, turn right. A little further along you will reach a left and right path. Turn left here, which is signed by a red waymarker. Almost immediately ignore the path on your left, also signed by a red waymarker, and continue straight ahead. You will reach a grass path. **❷** Turn right and then just after turn left, where you will pass an old wooden gatepost on your right. Almost immediately on reaching a fork, take the path on your left. You will pass amongst hazel coppice in this section of the wood. At the end of the path turn left and continue amongst the hazel.

On reaching a junction of paths, take the second left. On reaching another path, turn left and ascend gently. Ignore a path marked by a waymarker and continue. Just after you will reach a wide grass track. Turn right and continue along a woodland ride, which is floristic in the summer months. Another path joins the path which you are on from your left. **❸** Take this path. You will reach a boardwalk, where you will cross over a boggy section of the wood.

Cross a path which leads to a gate on your right, and continue straight ahead. On reaching another path, turn right. You will pass a path on your right just after, and then you will turn left on a path which is indicated by a waymarker. Descend into a dip, and then ascend again. Turn right just before a waymarker. Pass a path on your left and right. Continue straight ahead on the familiar path. On reaching the gate, put your dog on a lead, pass through the small gate and on reaching the road turn left. Continue on the road. You will soon reach your car.

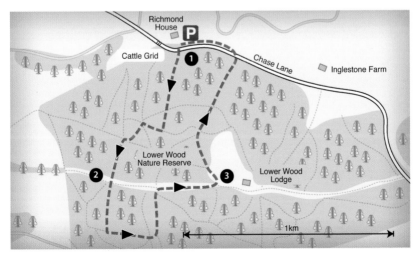

18. Prospect Stile

Med/Chall - 4.4 miles - 2 hrs

This wonderful circular walk ascends through open fields with mature parkland trees. For some of the walk, you will be between stock fences and hedgerows, where it is safe to have your dog off the lead. There is some open farmland, where there may be sheep grazing. You will pass through the beautiful, quiet village of North Stoke. On a clear day you will have lovely views in places. There are some gradual accents and some short sections of quiet country lane.

How to get there – This walk is located on edge of the Cotswolds, between Bath and Bristol, off the A431. On reaching Swineford, follow the brown sign for the car park and picnic area, which is at the side of the Swan pub.

Grid Reference – ST 690692

Nearest Postcode – BS30 6LN

Parking – Free

Facilities – There are no facilities

You will need – Dog lead, dog bags

The Walk

❶ From the car park, go back towards the road and take the footpath on your left, just before you reach the house on your left.
Pass the stone wall on your left with a stream within. Put your dog on a lead or under close control and go through the kissing gate.
Cross the field, veering slightly to your left, and head towards the telegraph pole.

Pass through the kissing gate on the other side of the field. Follow the sign for North Stoke and continue straight ahead across the field. Ascend gradually, and as you reach the trees turn around to appreciate the views. Pass through the kissing gate and continue on the bridleway between fences and mature trees.

Ascend gently to begin with, and then more steadily as you continue. The path becomes sunken, where you continue between wooded banks. As the gradient decreases, ignore a gap on your left, and just after turn right. You will reach and pass through a kissing gate. Continue on the narrow path between trees, with fields beyond on your left. There are views on your right, where the trees allow.

Turn a bend and ignore the path on your right. Continue straight ahead, beside a

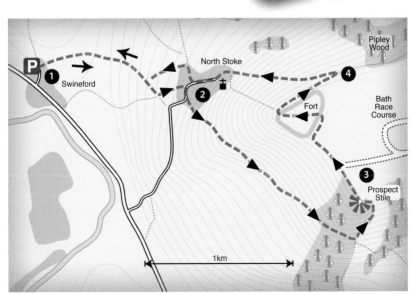

hedgerow and head towards a house, on the edge of a small field. Pass the house on your right and continue between the hedge and a high stone wall. Go through a kissing gate and continue between the fence and stone wall. On reaching a quiet road turn right. Continue through North Stoke village. As the road bends sharply to the right continue straight ahead and ascend on an access road. ❷

When you pass the last house on your left, the road becomes a track (bridleway). Continue to ascend between hedgerows. Descend to a gate, but don't go through it. Veer to your left and continue on the path, where you have views on your right. Continue between the stock fences, with views all around in places. Pass through a gate straight ahead of you, and continue to ascend between the trees.

Ignore a path on your right and one on your left, with a tall kissing gate, and continue straight ahead. On reaching another path, turn left. Go through the tall kissing gate, where you will now join part of the Cotswold Way long distance path. Continue straight ahead on the edge of Shiner's wood. Take a path which veers to your right, marked Cotswold Way. Continue between the hedgerows.

Ascend the steps and turn right onto another path. Continue to ascend. Pass through a tall kissing gate. The path bends sharply to your left and you will ascend steeply for a short section. ❸ On reaching a bench on your right, you will be rewarded with spectacular views on a clear day. Continue past the bench, put your dog on a lead, or under close control in case there are livestock, and go through a kissing gate. Be aware on race days there will be horses racing nearby. You will pass a topograph on your right. Turn left immediately after, following the Cotswold Way on the edge of the field.

You will reach and pass beside a white fence, which is part of the racecourse on your right. Soon after, pass through the kissing gate. Keep your dog under close control and continue on the edge of the field. There is a steep wooded slope on your left, beyond the barbed wire fence. There are some views here through gaps in the trees. As you turn around a corner in the field you will see a mound on your left, which is the remains of an ancient moat.

On reaching the end of the moat veer to your left, and continue through the middle of a large field of crops, and keep your dog on the path to avoid crop damage. There are views straight ahead. On reaching the end of the field, pass through a kissing gate. Keep your dog under close control or on a lead in case of livestock. Continue straight ahead and descend between the banks and beside the stock fence. On reaching the corner of the stock fence turn right, and continue on the Cotswold Way.

Continue on a level section of the field, which slopes steeply over on your left. Head for the gate in the field. Pass through the kissing gate and continue straight ahead, across another field. On reaching a stone track turn left. ❹

You have now left the Cotswold Way. Descend on the track which crosses the field, with views on your right. Pass through a gate and continue to descend on a quiet farm track between hedgerows and fields. Keep your dog under close control as the track leads into a farmyard ahead.

Ignore a footpath on your left just before the farm building, put your dog on a lead and continue towards the building. Pass a church on your left and the building on your right. Just after, pass a set of steps on your left. Your dog can access water on your left immediately after. Turn right, and continue to descend on the quiet lane through North Stoke once again. Just after you pass the post box on your right, which is inlaid into the wall, take the byway on your right, on the corner of Chestnut Barn.

After you pass the houses, continue around a left bend and continue on the quiet byway. After a short distance you will continue between trees. Ignore a path on your left. You are now in a familiar spot. Retrace your steps, and at the end of the path pass through the kissing gate, where you can enjoy views straight ahead. Descend across the fields and you will soon reach the car park.

19. Hanging Hill

Easy - 1.7 miles - 1hr

This is a fantastic short circular walk, located in Lansdown, which is close to the M4, Bath and Bristol. You will walk on part of the Cotswold Way, which is a long distance footpath. A quiet track beside a golf course brings you to sloping fields, which are floristic in the spring and summer months. Part of the walk follows a military history trail, and after a short ascent you will have wonderful views on a clear day. There may be cattle for a short section of the walk. There are two short sections of quiet country lanes, and you may come across horse riders, as some of the paths are bridleways.

How to get there – From the M4, turn off at junction 18, signed for the A46 Bath and Stroud. Follow the symbols on the brown signs for Bath Racecourse. Turn off the A46 and continue to follow the racecourse sign. On reaching another road, turn left, following the sign Lansdown 1 ½ miles. Soon after, as the road straightens you will see a verge on your left. Pass the lay-by and a road on your right opposite. Take the next narrow lane on your right. You will reach the small car park on your left, before going through the access gate.

Grid Reference – ST 719699   **Nearest Postcode** – BA1 9BZ

Parking – Small parking area (Keep gate access clear)

Facilities – There are no facilities

You will need – Dog lead, dog bags and water for your dog

The Walk

1 Take the bridleway, which is between the field gate and the gate across the access track. There is a stone wall on your left, with a field beyond it. On your right are mature beech trees. At the end of the path you will reach a fingerpost and a track beside a golf course, so keep your dog under close control.

2 Turn right on the track, following the sign for Cotswold Way bridlepath. Continue beside the golf course, with a stone wall and woodland on your right. Cross an access track and continue straight ahead. At the end of the golf course, take a path which veers to your right, signed Cotswolds Way. Go through a gate in the corner of a field, with the golf course on your right.

On a clear day there are extensive countryside views on your left. Keep your dog under close control or on a lead in case of livestock, and pass

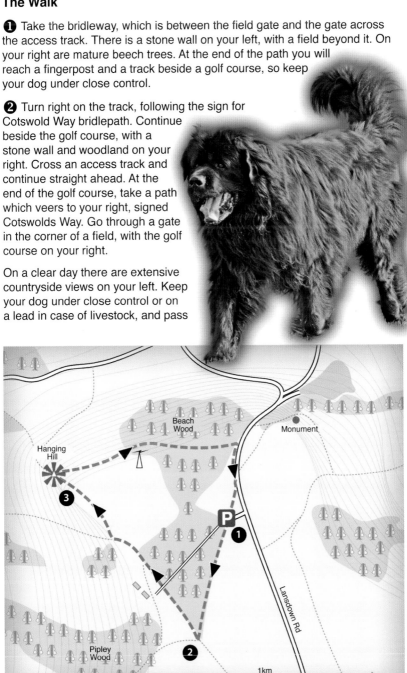

through a kissing gate where you leave the golf course behind. Continue on an undulating path between trees and scrub. The views continue where the trees clear. You will reach and continue on the edge of a field on your right. In the corner of the field you will reach a trig point, a flag for a military history trail and a kissing gate. ❸ Keep your dog on a lead or under close control, go through the kissing gate and turn right, where you will pass an interpretation panel with information on the Battle of Lansdown in 1643.

There are wonderful views on your left. Continue on the edge of a sloping field, which is known as 'Hanging Hill'. At the end of the field pass another flag and go through a gate. Continue on a path between trees. You will pass a fire depot on your right beyond a stone wall. Keep your dog under close control, as there is an access road ahead. Put your dog on a lead, and turn right on the road. At the end of the road go through a kissing gate on your left, where you will pass another flag.

Continue across a woodland ride, with a road over on your right. As you continue, you will reach close to the road. Put your dog on a lead if you think it will pass through the wire fence on your right. You will reach a gate. Put your dog on a lead, go through the gate, and turn left on the quiet road. There's a busy road which runs parallel with the road you are on. When you reach another flag, ignore the path on your left and continue straight ahead. Immediately before you reach the main road, take a path on your right. Cross through the middle of a crop/hay field (corner to corner), where you will reach back to your car.

20. Winsley

Med/Chall - 1.5 miles - 1hr 30min

This is a wonderful circular walk. Part of the walk is beside the Avon Canal. As you leave the canal you will cross an aqueduct. There is a gradual but long ascent through woodland and then across farmland. Continue on quiet footpaths, where you will reach back into the village of Winsley.

How to get there – From Bath, take the A36 following the signs for Warminster. On reaching Limpley Stoke turn left following the sign for Bradford -on-Avon, Lower Limpley Stoke and Winsley on the B3108. On reaching Lower Limpley continue to follow directions for Winsley. Soon after, on reaching Winsley, continue on the road, and turn right where you see the small sign for Murhill. Continue on the narrow lane, where you will see the car park on your right.

Grid Reference – ST 793 607

Nearest Postcode – BA2 7FG

Parking – Free in the car park on Murhill

Facilities – There are no facilities

You will need – Dog lead, dog bags

The Walk

❶ From the car park, face the road and turn right. Just after the car park, and as you reach the stone wall on your right, turn right. Descend the steps and then descend on the private access road on your left, which is quite steep to begin with. You will pass several driveways, and then the road becomes a path between trees. You will reach Avon Canal. Continue beside the canal on your right. Before you reach a canal bridge, put your dog on a lead. ❷ Ascend the steps and then turn right. Cross the canal bridge and then turn left on the towpath. Keep your dog under close control, as cyclists use the towpath.

Before the canal bends sharply to your right, where you see the white metal fence ahead, put your dog on a lead, as there is a wall with a considerable drop on the other side. You will then cross a railway bridge and aqueduct. After you have crossed the aqueduct, descend two sets of steps on your right. Continue under the arch of the aqueduct. Ascend on the path and then turn right before the pub. Ascend and then turn right, keep your dog on a lead and cross the aqueduct and railway bridge.

Winsley

Limpley Stoke Rd

Bradford Rd

❹

Turleigh

P ❶

❷

❸

Avoncliff Station

Kennet and Avon Canal

River Avon   Avoncliff

Avoncliff Wood

1km

You will pass a car park on your left, where you continue straight ahead on a footpath into woodland. ❸ Almost immediately, ignore the footpath on your left and continue straight ahead. Ascend the steps, go through a kissing gate, and put your dog on a lead or under close control, as there may be cattle grazing. If there is an electric fence beside the path, put your dog on a lead. Continue straight ahead on the obvious worn path, ascending gently through the field. On reaching the field boundary, turn left and continue on the field edge, with a hedgerow on your right. You will ascend quite steeply, and on reaching the corner of the field, cross a track and continue straight ahead. Pass through a kissing gate, and continue to ascend steeply on a path between a hedgerow and stone wall.

On reaching the end of the path, put your dog on a lead and go between the squeeze stones. Continue straight ahead on the access track, which later becomes a road. ❹ Just before you reach a sharp left hand bend in the road, take the footpath on your left and pass between the squeeze stones. Continue between the stone walls. At the end of the path, go between the squeeze stones and descend the steps. Ignore a path on your left and continue straight ahead, with the stone wall on your right and a stock fence on your left, with a narrow field beyond.

As you continue to descend there are views on your left and ahead. As you pass the narrow field on your left put your dog on a lead, as there's a road ahead. On reaching the end of the path, go to the right of the gate. Turn right on the quiet road and continue through the village of Winsley. Ascend to the end of the road, and then turn left. You will soon reach the car park on your left.

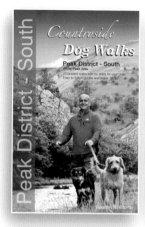

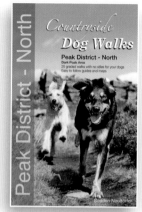

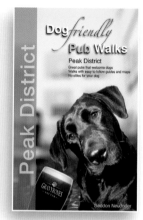

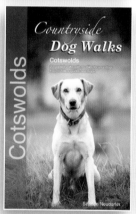

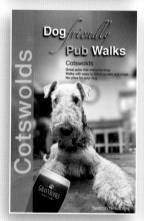

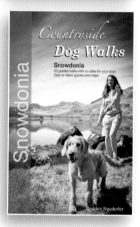

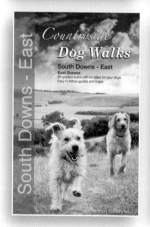

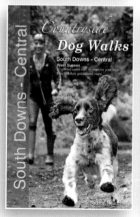

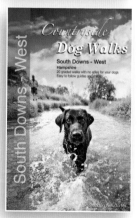

www.countrysidedogwalks.co.uk

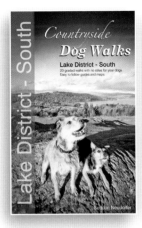

Lake District - South

Countryside
Dog Walks
Lake District - South
20 graded walks with no stiles for your dogs.
Easy to follow guides and maps.
Seddon Neudorfer

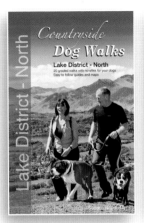

Lake District - North

Countryside
Dog Walks
Lake District - North
20 graded walks with no stiles for your dogs.
Easy to follow guides and maps.
Seddon Neudorfer

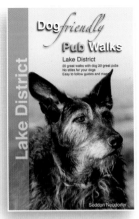

Lake District

Dog*friendly*
Pub Walks
Lake District
20 great walks with dog 20 great pubs
No stiles for your dogs
Easy to follow guides and maps
Seddon Neudorfer

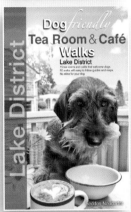

Lake District

Dog*friendly*
Tea Room & Café Walks
Lake District
15 tea rooms and cafés that welcome dogs
PC walks with easy to follow guides and maps.
No stiles for your dog
Seddon Neudorfer

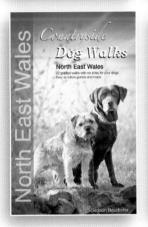

North East Wales

Countryside
Dog Walks
North East Wales
20 graded walks with no stiles for your dogs
Easy to follow guides and maps.
Seddon Neudorfer

Greater Manchester

Countryside
Dog Walks
Greater Manchester
20 graded walks with no stiles for your dogs.
Easy to follow guides and maps.
Seddon Neudorfer

Wirral & West Cheshire

Countryside
Dog Walks
Wirral & West Cheshire
20 graded walks with no stiles for your dogs
Easy to follow guides and maps.
Seddon Neudorfer

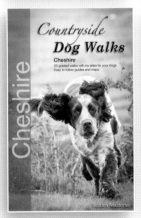

Cheshire

Countryside
Dog Walks
Cheshire
20 graded walks with no stiles for your dogs
Easy to follow guides and maps.
Seddon Neudorfer

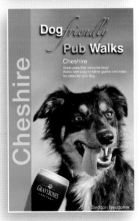

Cheshire

Dog*friendly*
Pub Walks
Cheshire
Great pubs that welcome dogs
Walks with easy to follow guides and maps
No stiles for your dog
Seddon Neudorfer

Follow us on Facebook for progress reports on our future publications.

Search - Countryside Dog Walks

Wet Nose Publishing Ltd

90

Home Made Dog Treats
Recipe Book

Seddon Neudorfer

New Release Nov - 2016

Simple recipes made from ingredients in your kitchen

Healthy ingredients to ensure a healthy dog

Fun and easy to make

Wet Nose
Publishing Ltd

"Cooking treats is easy"